Issues today

Citizenship and Identity

Contents

A resource for KS3

About Key Stage 3

Key Stage 3 refers to the first three years of secondary schooling, normally years 7, 8 and 9, during which pupils are aged between 11 and 14.

This series is also suitable for Scottish P7, S1 and S2 students.

About Issues Today

Issues Today is a series of resource books on contemporary social issues for Key Stage 3 pupils. It is based on the concept behind the popular *Issues* series for 14- to 18-year-olds, also published by Independence.

Each volume contains information from a variety of sources, including government reports and statistics, newspaper and magazine articles, surveys and polls, academic research and literature from charities and lobby groups. The information has been tailored to an 11 to 14 age group; it has been rewritten and presented in a simple, straightforward format to be accessible to Key Stage 3 pupils.

In addition, each *Issues Today* title features handy tasks and assignments based on the information contained in the book, for use in class, for homework or as a revision aid.

Issues Today can be used as a learning resource in a variety of Key Stage 3 subjects, including English, Science, History, Geography, PSHE, Citizenship, Sex and Relationships Education and Religious Education.

About this book

Citizenship and Identity is the thirty-second volume in the *Issues Today* series. It looks at what it means to be British and explores how our democracy works. Modern Britain is a diverse, multicultural society, in which the concept of 'Britishness' is difficult to define. Do UK citizens share a common national identity? What rights and responsibilities do British citizens have and what role do they play in the way the country is governed?

Citizenship and Identity offers a useful overview of the many issues involved in this topic. However, at the end of each article is a URL for the relevant organisation's website, which can be visited by pupils who want to carry out further research.

Because the information in this book is gathered from a number of different sources, pupils should think about the origin of the text and critically evaluate the information that is presented. Does the source have a particular bias or agenda? Are you being presented with facts or opinions? Do you agree with the writer?

At the end of each chapter there are two pages of activities relating to the articles and issues raised in that chapter. The 'Brainstorm' questions can be done as a group or individually after reading the articles. This should prompt some ideas and lead on to further activities. Some suggestions for such activities are given under the headings 'Oral', 'Moral Dilemmas', 'Research', 'Written' and 'Design' that follow the 'Brainstorm' questions.

For more information about *Issues Today* and its sister series, *Issues* (for pupils aged 14 to 18), please visit the Independence website.

www.independence.co.uk

What does citizenship mean?

A legal and political status

In its simplest meaning, 'citizenship' is used to refer to the status of being a citizen – that is, to being a member of a particular political community or state. Citizenship in this sense brings with it certain rights and responsibilities that are defined in law, such as the right to vote, the responsibility to pay tax and so on. It is sometimes referred to as nationality, and is what is meant when someone talks about 'applying for', 'getting', or being 'refused' citizenship.

Involvement in public life and affairs

The term 'citizenship' is also used to refer to involvement in public life and affairs – that is, to the behaviour and actions of a citizen. It is sometimes known as active citizenship. Citizenship in this sense is applied to a wide range of activities – from voting in elections and standing for political office to taking an interest in politics and current affairs. It refers not only to rights and responsibilities laid down in the law, but also to general forms of behaviour – social and moral – which societies expect of their citizens. What these rights, responsibilities and forms of behaviour should be is an area of ongoing public debate, with people holding a range of views.

The term 'citizenship' has several different meanings:

An educational activity

Finally, 'citizenship' is used to refer to an educational activity – that is, to the process of helping people learn how to become active, informed and responsible citizens. Citizenship in this sense is also known as citizenship education or education for citizenship. It encompasses all forms of education, from informal education in the home or through youth work to more formal types of education provided in schools, colleges, universities, training organisations and the workplace. At the formal end of the spectrum, it gives its name both to a distinct subject in the National Curriculum for 11- to 16-year-olds and to a general area of study leading to an academic qualification – both of which, confusingly, are sometimes spelled with a small and sometimes a capital 'c'.

Reprinted from 'Making Sense of Citizenship: A Continuing Professional Development Handbook' by Young Citizens Passport (Hodder Murray, 2006), published by Hodder Education in association with the Citizenship Foundation. Reproduced by permission of John Murray (Publishers) Ltd.
© Hodder Education

www.citizenshipfoundation.org.uk

National ceremonies and symbols

THE UNION FLAG, THE NATIONAL ANTHEM, currency, stamps and other national events help identify and symbolise what it is to be British and to live in the United Kingdom.

Flags

The Union Flag, or 'Union Jack', is the national flag of the United Kingdom and is so called because it includes the flags of the three countries united under one Sovereign – the kingdoms of England and Wales, of Scotland and of Ireland (although since 1921 only Northern Ireland, rather than the whole of Ireland, has been part of the United Kingdom).

The term 'Union Jack' possibly dates from Queen Anne's time (reigned 1702-14), but its origin is uncertain.

The Royal Standard represents the Sovereign and the United Kingdom. The Royal Standard is flown when the Queen is in residence in one of the Royal Palaces, on the Queen's car on official journeys and on aircraft. It may also be flown on any building, official or private (but not ecclesiastical buildings), during a visit by the Queen.

Mini glossary

Sovereign – *king or queen*

ecclesiastical – *of or relating to a church*

patriotic – *love of or devotion to one's country*

anonymous – *by someone whose name and identity are unknown*

seal – *a design imprinted in wax to authenticate a document*

regalia – *symbols of royalty*

www.direct.gov.uk

The above information is reprinted with kind permission from Directgov.
© Crown copyright

National anthem

'God Save the King' was a patriotic song first publicly performed in London in 1745, which came to be referred to as the National Anthem from the beginning of the nineteenth century. The words and tune are anonymous, and may date back to the seventeenth century. There is no authorised version of the National Anthem as the words are a matter of tradition.

Ceremonies

The armed forces are involved in many of the great ceremonies of state, such as trooping the colours, the state opening of Parliament, Remembrance Sunday and state visits.

Currency, coins and banknotes

The Bank of England has issued banknotes since it was founded in 1694. The Royal Mint can be traced back more than a thousand years and its main responsibility is to make and distribute United Kingdom coins.

Stamps

The Royal Mail publishes stamps for the UK. Symbols of the royal origins of the UK's postal system remain: a miniature silhouette of the Monarch's head is depicted on all stamps.

Great Seal

The Great Seal of the Realm is the chief seal of the Crown, used to show the monarch's approval of important state documents.

Royal Coat of Arms

The Royal Coat of Arms identifies the person who is Head of State. In the UK, the royal arms are borne only by the Sovereign. They are used in many ways in connection with the administration and government of the country, for instance on coins, in churches and on public buildings.

The Crown Jewels

The crowns and treasures associated with the British Monarchy are powerful symbols of monarchy. For over 600 years kings and queens of England have stored crowns, robes and other valuable items of ceremonial regalia at the Tower of London. Since the 17th century, at least, this collection has been known as the 'Crown Jewels'.

British identity

IN THE LAST DECADES OF THE TWENTIETH CENTURY, there was a decline in the proportion of people in Great Britain who thought of themselves as primarily or exclusively British and a growing proportion of people who thought of themselves as Scottish, Welsh or English (or none of these) rather than British.

A sense of British identity nevertheless remains widespread and in all three territories the majority of British residents continue to have dual identities, as both British and Scottish, British and Welsh or British and English. A small but growing number (around 10%) of people reject all four national identities.

> *Britons tend to feel proud of being British, and levels of national pride are higher than in most other countries in the EU15.*

National pride

Britons tend to feel proud of being British, and levels of national pride are higher than in most other countries in the EU15. In contrast, levels of attachment or sense of belonging to Britain is below the European average.

There is evidence of decline over the last two decades in strength of national pride (although largely from 'very strong' to 'fairly strong' sense of pride) and there may well have been a modest decline in attachment too.

By Professor Anthony Heath and Jane Roberts

Mini glossary

decline – become smaller; fall

dual – consisting of two parts

EU15 – The 15 countries belonging to the European Union (up until 2004 when more countries joined the EU)

modest – fairly small

www.justice.gov.uk

Attachment to Britain

► The main driver of a feeling of attachment or belonging to Britain is age, with younger people being less strongly attached to Britain. It is likely that much of the decline in pride and attachment is due to younger generations, who feel a lower sense of attachment, gradually replacing older generations.

► Controlling for age, we find no evidence that Muslims or people of Pakistani heritage were in general less attached to Britain than were other religions or ethnic groups. Ethnic minorities show clear evidence of 'dual' rather than 'exclusive' identities. However, people born overseas in a non-Commonwealth country and people who have arrived in Britain only recently tend to have a weaker sense of belonging to Britain.

► Socio-economic marginality (lower social class or low income, or a limiting long-term illness) is associated with slightly weaker feelings of belonging.

► Among young people born in Britain, the lack of attachment of Black Caribbeans is especially marked, reaching one-third or more. This applies to the second generation as well as to the first, migrant generation.

► A feeling of belonging or attachment to Britain appears to be associated with social trust, a sense of civic duty (at least as indicated by turnout in elections) and by increased support for the current political order.

► A sense of belonging to Britain is not associated with particularly xenophobic attitudes, nor is it associated with distinctive political positions (other than on European integration and maintenance of the union).

► Policies should, perhaps, be considered which address the weak sense of belonging on the part of people born overseas in non-Commonwealth countries, of second-generation minorities (especially those of Caribbean heritage) and of the economically marginal.

► Any reforms need to consider not only how to strengthen British identity but also what form of identity should be encouraged.

Strong sense of belonging

PEOPLE FEEL THEIR LOCAL AREA *is a place where individuals from different backgrounds get on well together, new figures show.*

▶ Figures from the citizenship survey show that 82 per cent of people see their community as cohesive, an increase from 80 per cent in 2005;

▶ 76 per cent of people feel that they strongly belong to their neighbourhood, with 81 per cent of people satisfied with their local area as a place to live;

▶ older people were more likely to be satisfied with their local area than younger people (88 per cent of people aged 75 years and over).

The survey is less positive on people feeling their voices are being heard at a local level. Fewer than 40 per cent of respondents felt able to influence decisions in their local area. This is an area the Government is keen to address and has set out plans which will go even further in giving more power to local people.

These findings come from The Citizenship Survey: April-September 2008 (covering the first two quarters of data from the 2008-09 survey).

> ❝ *76 per cent of people feel that they strongly belong to their neighbourhood.* ❞

Every year almost 15,000 people are asked for their views on issues around community cohesion, discrimination, values, civic engagement and interaction. The biggest survey of its kind in the UK, the survey is one of the key tools used by Government to measure the effect of its policies. The full survey is available on the Communities and Local Government website.

Cohesion Minister Sadiq Khan said:

❝ Britain has a proud history of individuals from different backgrounds living side by side with each other and as this survey shows there remains more uniting us than dividing us.

We must not take this for granted though. We need to ensure that Britain continues to be a place where people are proud to live and everyone can succeed. That means building on what we have already done to deliver equal opportunities and racial equality.

Too few people feel they can influence decisions either at a local or national level. This is something we must address and why we are giving people more power to have a greater say in the way that local decisions that affect them are made. ❞

Key findings

Community cohesion and belonging

▶ 76 per cent of people felt they belonged strongly to their neighbourhood, an increase from 70 per cent in 2003;

▶ 81 per cent of people were satisfied with their local area as a place to live;

▶ older people were more likely to be satisfied with their local area than younger people. Levels of satisfaction were highest among those aged 75 years and over (88 per cent) and lowest among those aged 16 to 24 years old (76 per cent);

▶ 81 per cent of people mixed socially at least once a month with people from different ethnic or religious backgrounds.

Strong sense of belonging

Active and empowered communities

▶ 39 per cent of people feel they can influence decisions affecting their local area. 22 per cent feel they could influence decisions affecting Great Britain. Both measures remain unchanged since 2007/08 but both have fallen since 2001;

▶ 41 per cent of adults have volunteered formally at least once in the 12 months prior to interview.

Discrimination

▶ 10 per cent of people said that racial or religious harassment was a big problem in their local area. A higher proportion of people from minority ethnic groups (20 per cent) thought that racial or religious harassment was a problem compared to White people (nine per cent);

▶ Eight per cent of people from minority ethnic groups felt they had been refused a job for reasons of race compared with two per cent of white people who felt they were refused a job on these grounds.

29 January 2009

❝❝ **Britain has a proud history of individuals from different backgrounds living side by side with each other and as this survey shows there remains more uniting us than dividing us.** ❞❞

www.communities.gov.uk

The above information is reprinted with kind permission from the Department for Communities and Local Government.
© Crown copyright

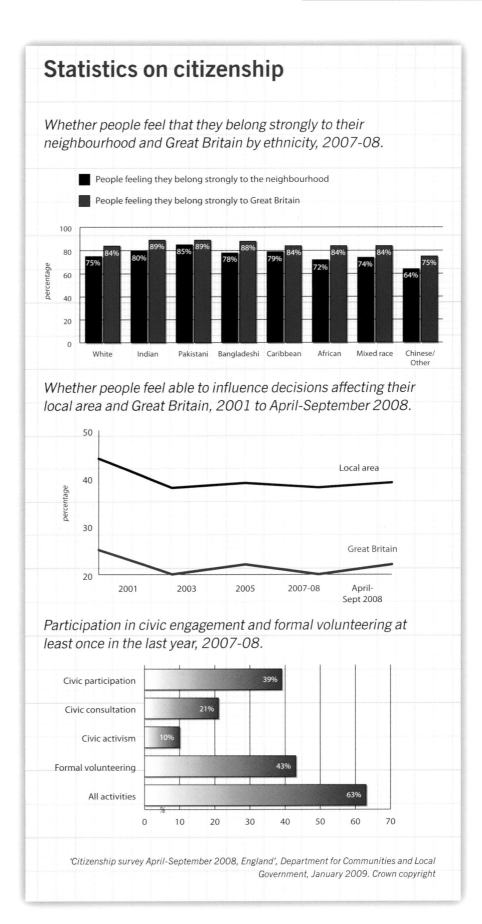

Statistics on citizenship

Whether people feel that they belong strongly to their neighbourhood and Great Britain by ethnicity, 2007-08.

■ People feeling they belong strongly to the neighbourhood
■ People feeling they belong strongly to Great Britain

	Neighbourhood	Great Britain
White	75%	84%
Indian	80%	89%
Pakistani	85%	89%
Bangladeshi	78%	88%
Caribbean	79%	84%
African	72%	84%
Mixed race	74%	84%
Chinese/Other	64%	75%

Whether people feel able to influence decisions affecting their local area and Great Britain, 2001 to April-September 2008.

Local area

Great Britain

2001   2003   2005   2007-08   April-Sept 2008

Participation in civic engagement and formal volunteering at least once in the last year, 2007-08.

Civic participation	39%
Civic consultation	21%
Civic activism	10%
Formal volunteering	43%
All activities	63%

0   10   20   30   40   50   60   70

'Citizenship survey April-September 2008, England', Department for Communities and Local Government, January 2009. Crown copyright

Britishness and social cohesion

TRYING TO CREATE a fixed sense of 'Britishness' will not achieve social cohesion.

Addressing deprivation and how people connect is more important for social cohesion than trying to get everyone to adhere to the same fixed notion of 'Britishness'. This is according to research published by the Joseph Rowntree Foundation. The report also found that limited opportunities for British people in parts of the UK are undermining attempts to ensure new migrants are well received. It found a stark divide between places that are equipped to adapt to new migrants, and places that are not.

The research found that many people valued their children growing up with cultural diversity. However, some felt that their, and their children's, prospects were reduced because of immigration – particularly when it came to housing and education.

> **Lead Researcher Professor Mary Hickman, Director of the Institute for the Study of European Transformations (ISET) at London Metropolitan University, said:**
>
> ❝ We found that although many British people value the UK for being multi-ethnic and multicultural, poverty and lack of opportunities undermine social cohesion, especially in certain parts of our towns and cities. A key factor influencing whether new migrants are accepted is the dominant story in each locality about who belongs there. ❞

Communities who saw their locality as belonging to everyone tended to be more open to new arrivals. Whereas communities who thought of a locality as belonging to them in particular were more likely to blame new arrivals for problems that often already existed.

The report also looked at feelings of Britishness among both the settled UK population and new migrants in England, Scotland and Northern Ireland. It found that minority ethnic long-term residents and new arrivals were the most positive about what was good about Britain.

White English people who were questioned often found it difficult to reflect on their feelings of belonging to Britain, because they had not previously considered it. Whereas people in Scotland and Northern Ireland felt they belonged more to their respective nations than to Britain.

The authors conclude: 'The findings of this research go against the grain of the idea that we need a fixed notion of Britishness and British values. Rather, "cohesion" is about negotiating the right balance between difference and unity.'

This press release summarises information from the Joseph Rowntree Foundation report *Immigration and social cohesion in the UK* by Mary Hickman, Helen Crowley and Nick Mai.

21 July 2008

Mini glossary

deprivation – extreme poverty

adhere – act in accordance with

undermine – weaken

dominant – most common; having the most influence

www.jrf.org.uk

Britain and beyond

BETWEEN MAY AND JULY 2008, YouthNet carried out research to explore young peoples' attitudes towards diversity in the UK, European citizenship and issues such as immigration, multiculturalism, integration and racism.

This project was funded by the Youth in Action Programme. Using an online survey and an online focus group discussion, YouthNet consulted with more than 850 young people from across the UK aged between 16 and 24.

British and European identities

▶ The focus group participants were fairly ambivalent about being described as British and did not readily relate to a shared British identity. They were, however, conscious of the nations which made up the UK, both culturally and in terms of personal identity.

▶ For many of the young focus group participants, the concept of 'Britishness' consisted of a variety of cultural stereotypes and associations, both positive and negative. They identified more readily with the idea of accepting change and difference, which some perceived to be a British quality.

▶ Around half (51%) of the survey respondents said they feel European; however, the vast majority (74%) thought that the UK was very different to the rest of Europe.

▶ Perceived cultural differences, more than geography, dissuaded many young British people from identifying as European. These included food, eating habits, art and a difference in attitudes on the continent to binge drinking.

▶ Nearly half (46%) of the survey respondents considered themselves to have good knowledge of European cultures, having acquired it from friends, holidays and the media. Only a quarter (27%) thought that young people were taught a lot about other European cultures at school.

www.youthnet.org

Going abroad

▶ Nearly nine in ten (87%) young British people who took part in the survey had visited countries in Europe outside of the UK. Over half (56%) had been abroad beyond Europe.

▶ Three out of five (62%) survey respondents believed that Europeans were welcoming to British visitors, and two in five (44%) said that the British were not discriminated against in European cultures.

▶ A significant minority (13%) of respondents said that Europeans were not welcoming to British visitors, and some focus group participants believed that being British, or moreover English, was the reason for negative attitudes towards them.

▶ Less than half (46%) of the survey respondents spoke a European language other than English and many felt that language barriers caused difficulties for them in European countries.

Influencing UK attitudes to Europe

▶ On the whole, the young British people who took part in the research were not anti-Europe or the EU; however, most felt that UK media coverage of the issues was largely negative.

▶ Focus group participants were concerned that negative media stories about Europe unfairly influence people's attitudes and create hostility towards the EU and immigration, and encourage racist behaviour.

▶ Many were hopeful about the future of the UK's relationship with Europe and the EU, although they were concerned about widespread ignorance and negativity about the issues. They suggested schools, the media and the Government could address this.

> **Mini glossary**
>
> **ambivalent** – *uncertain; having conflicting feelings about something*
>
> **concept** – *idea*
>
> **significant** – *fairly large number*

The above information is an extract from the YouthNet research 'Britain and beyond' and is reprinted with permission. © YouthNet

Just who do we think we are?

A REVIEW PUBLISHED BY THE former attorney general Lord Goldsmith said that more than a third of young black Britons feel no sense of attachment to Britain, while a further one in ten people said they rejected all four identities of British, English, Scottish or Welsh.

Among other ways to enhance British bonds, Goldsmith suggested extending citizenship ceremonies to all 18-year-olds, with an oath of allegiance to the Queen or to the country. Across the country the *Guardian* went on to the streets to ask how British people think they are.

... Jermyn Street

On Jermyn Street, leaning on his cane a thimble's throw from Piccadilly, stands a bronze statue of icon George 'Beau' Brummell. His personal and very British belief – 'To be truly elegant one should not be noticed' – is engraved on the plinth beneath his boots. And while it may be hard to know what Brummell would have made of Lord Goldsmith's proposals, the shoppers and vendors of Jermyn Street had their own ideas.

'Getting children of 18 to swear allegiance to the Queen is a gimmick,' said John Bray outside his menswear shop. 'The trouble with this country is that the politicians are like advertising men: they're trained to lie with enthusiasm.'

Bray, 73, describes himself as 'very much British' and feels that a sense of national identity is best forged at home. 'It would be much better if the parents brought them up in all aspects of life,' he said. 'My wife is Polish and I spend quite a lot of time in Poland. The children over there treat their elders very differently from the way they do here. Education starts at home.'

Felix Cole, 49, a financial adviser, was equally uncharitable about some elements of the citizenship review – especially the debated oath. 'I thought it was nuts,' he said. 'It's an American idea and I don't think it would work here. I just feel that it's every parent's job to bring up their kids and give them personality and character and show them the country they're living in. It's not the state's responsibility.'

Walking past Turnbull & Asser was Jane Brackfield, who had more time for the oath, but had reservations about the wording and what young people would think about it. 'It would be very nice if people did it with their families because families are a big thing in this country.'

'I think we mustn't be afraid to let people practise what they want to practise,' she said. 'I've got no problems with people celebrating other things but I don't feel that I should be ashamed of saying I'm a Christian. It would be nice if we could have Muslims, Jews and Christians all saying the same thing and swearing allegiance to the country they live in and embracing it.'

Colin Barlow, 55, a motorcycle taxi driver from Kent, thought about Britain and Britishness as he waited for a fare outside Dolce & Gabbana on Old Bond Street. 'I think it's going to the dogs,' he said. 'We're losing our identity and there's less pride in being British these days. It's a very slow process; these things don't just stop, but politeness is disappearing a bit and people are getting a bit more aggressive.'

'The Americans, for example, have a culture of being proud of being American, and if we had that, it would be better.' He was, however, in no doubt as to his own identity. 'I'm English,' he said. 'I've always lived here and I can't speak Welsh – or understand the Scots.'

By Sam Jones

Just who do we think we are?

Bradford

Three union flags were hanging high over Bradford's Centenary Square, wrapping themselves limply round their poles in the way that the emblem of the country is apt to do. Down below, enthusiasm for a post-school oath of allegiance was equally lukewarm, but not because of any hesitations about feeling naturally British.

'It's just that there's no point in it. I think it's a waste of time,' said chef Ali Umma, 30. 'Wasting public money, too. We're already running a good system as it is, so why do they need to introduce new things like this?'

He and his friends on a lunch break accepted there were problems between communities, but he said: 'Which country doesn't have those? We can solve them, maybe quicker if we use the money they'd be wasting on this allegiance thing.'

Royalty was likely to be a particular sticking point for younger people, as older ones in the square acknowledged. Susan Rhodes, retired from a career in social care, said: 'You wouldn't get young people to do it. Maybe in our day, but times have changed.'

Three students from Bradford College worried that the suggested ceremony could be more divisive than helpful. Laura Barker, 17, said: 'It's just going to divide people more, because the ones that will swear allegiance are going to be mad at people that don't, or don't want to. They're going to have to make it like you have a choice, because so many people will just leave if you have to do it.'

Her friend Chantelle Brooking, also 17, agreed and echoed Umma: 'We've got on so well before without it, so why bother? People are going to unify whether we have an oath of allegiance or not. It's not any symbol that's going to bring us together, it's people getting together.'

By Martin Wainwright

Stirling

When Audrey Ferrand was looking for a name for her luxury Scottish goods shop in the centre of Stirling, she wanted something that reflected her identity as a Scot and a Briton. She chose Thistle & Rose. Ferrand, 42, who was born in South Lanarkshire, lived and worked in London and Paris for 15 years before returning to Scotland with her French husband to raise their children.

'I think I would say I am British first and then definitely Scottish – probably the Scottish side has got a stronger feel to it. Scottish people have always been proud of being Scottish, but I don't think devolution or the parliament has made a great difference to us, in terms of having an even stronger identity. We are still British first.' Ferrand said she would accept that the notion of Britishness had faded in recent years but did not believe that the government could counter it with initiatives such as a national day or an oath of allegiance to Queen and country.

James Mackay, 55, from Dunkeld, a retired RAF flight engineer, spent 23 years in the air force and worked on the Queen's Flight, including the monarch's 1991 visit to Africa. As a member of the armed forces he was required to swear an oath of allegiance, and had no issue with doing so. But he is strongly opposed to ministers intervening to promote the notion of Britishness, particularly making school leavers swear an oath of allegiance to Queen or country. Mackay said he was a Scot who was proud to be British, but suspected that many Scots would resist efforts by Westminster to cultivate a renewed sense of Britishness. 'I don't think this whole thing will go down very well here,' he said. 'It is a very nationalistic country, Scotland.'

Roy Smith, 42, an auxiliary nurse at Stirling Royal Infirmary, said: 'I'm Scottish. If you go to America and people say, 'oh you're English,' I always correct them. But if someone was to call me British it would not bother me,' he said. 'And I don't think there is really a problem about Britishness. The politicians are thinking too much about it. We have a multicultural society now, which is a good thing about the UK. We should focus on that.'

By Kirsty Scott

Just who do we think we are?

Thetford

The Norfolk market town of Thetford is home to an estimated 10,000 Portuguese drawn to East Anglia by the promise of well-paid work on the farms, in fields and in the factories.

Most have arrived in the past seven years to begin a new life in a community of Norfolk locals and London overspill.

Bar manager Helder Lopez – whose pub was attacked by stone-throwing white locals after Portugal knocked England out of the World Cup two years ago – said: 'I have been here seven years and I consider myself British. I have two young sons and a daughter and they all speak English as well as Portuguese. I would be happy for them to take an oath of allegiance to this country but the final choice will have to be theirs.'

'But too many people come here thinking it is easy street – and for many that turns out to be true. I know people from Europe who have come to this town and haven't had a job in five years. For them it is a land of milk and honey, but for the rest of us it has sometimes been a struggle. Most of us have learned the language so we can feel included in the life here yet too often the scroungers don't do anything and don't join in.'

Joao de Noronha is editor of a Thetford-based Portuguese newspaper published fortnightly with a national circulation of more than 20,000 – 2,000 copies of which are sold in Thetford. He believes language is the barrier to closer integration of the Portuguese in Thetford. He says most of the under-30s arrive – especially those of school age – and learn English quickly. But he admits the older generations, some of whom have been here for seven years, are not prepared to change.

He has helped to set up European Challenge, an organisation dedicated to helping new arrivals settle in the area by offering translation and interpretation services and practical guidance to bureaucracy in the UK.

Naronha, 57, said: 'There is a problem with language which we are trying to address and it has been a barrier. Older people do not see themselves as included and they do not wish to be. But the younger ones want to be included so they have mixed emotions.

'Most of us would have no problem with swearing an oath of allegiance – this country is now their home and they do not want to go back to Portugal.'

Not everyone in Thetford, however, sees the benefits of the mass immigration. Derek Antrobus and his wife, Maureen, moved to the town 34 years ago to escape city life in the north of England. In that time they say they have seen plenty of change – enough for them to claim they feel like foreigners in their own land.

Mrs Antrobus, 57, said: 'I feel we are now in a minority here. Walking through the town all you hear is foreigners – they have their own shops, pubs and cafes, which is not a bad thing. I have got some Portuguese friends but it is not the same sleepy Norfolk town it was when we arrived.'

By Richard Goss

15 March 2008

Mini glossary

oath – *a promise*

unify – *bring together*

cultivate – *develop*

gimmick – *something that will attract publicity*

bureaucracy – *government systems and regulations*

Citizenship tests

SINCE 1 NOVEMBER 2005 everyone that wants to permanently live in the UK has to take a test or attend citizenship and language classes to prove that they know about life in the UK.

The Home Office said it wanted to create a new, more meaningful, way of becoming a citizen to help people share British values and traditions.

The subjects in the test are:

1. A Changing Society (migration, the role of women, children, family and young people);

2. UK Today: A Profile (population, the nations and regions of the UK, religion, customs and traditions);

3. How the United Kingdom is governed (the British constitution, the UK in Europe and the world);

4. Everyday needs (housing, services in and for the home, money and credit, health, education, leisure, travel and transport);

5. Employment (looking for work, equal rights and discrimination, at work, working for yourself, childcare and children at work).

> *This is not a test of someone's ability to be British or a test of their Britishness.*

Tom McNulty, the Immigration Minister at the time the tests were introduced said:

> This is not a test of someone's ability to be British or a test of their Britishness. It is a test of their preparedness to become citizens, in keeping with the language requirement as well. It is about looking forward, rather than an assessment of their ability to understand history.

The test is made up of 24 questions which have to be answered in 45 minutes in English. You need to get 18 out of the 24 questions right to become a British Citizen – would you?

October 2008

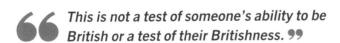
www.headsup.org.uk

The above information is reprinted with kind permission from HeadsUp!
© Hansard Society

Mini glossary

migration – moving from one country to another

constitution – laws and principles by which the UK is governed

discrimination – treating a person or group of people unfairly because of their race, colour, nationality, ethnic or national origin

Activities

Brainstorm

Brainstorm to find out what you know about citizenship and national identity.

1. What is citizenship?

   ....

   ....

   ....

2. Write your own definition of the term 'Britishness.'

   ....

   ....

   ....

Oral activities

3. Look at the article *National ceremonies and symbols* on page 2. In a group, come up with a list of things that you feel represent modern Britain.

   NOTES..

   ....

   ....

4. Prepare a talk for your class about your local neighbourhood and community. Describe how united you feel your community is, thinking about any events and activities that bring local people together.

   NOTES..

   ....

Moral Dilemmas

5. Imagine that you are a politician voting on whether young British citizens should have to swear an oath of allegiance to the Queen. How would you vote and why?

6. If you had to define yourself either as British, or as belonging only to the country you were born in (e.g. England, Scotland, Northern Ireland, Wales or a country outside Britain), which identity would you choose? Explain your answer.

Activities

Research activities

7. Read the article *Just who do we think we are?* on pages 8-10. Interview some people in your area to find out how British they feel they are. Do you notice any trends in the answers of people of different ages?

   CONCLUSIONS..

   ....

   ....

   ....

8. Find out about Australia Day, the national celebration of being Australian which takes place each year. Come up with some ideas for a similar day which would celebrate Britain. Think about when the day should be held and what the celebrations would consist of. Do you think having a 'Britain Day' is a good idea?

   NOTES..

   ....

   ....

   ....

Written activities

Complete the following activities in your exercise books or on a sheet of paper.

9. Read the article *Citizenship tests* on page 11. Write a set of questions that you feel should be included on a test like this. Do you think citizenship tests are a good idea? Why, or why not?

10. Write the lyrics for a new national anthem for the United Kingdom. The lyrics should reflect life in the UK today.

Design activities

11. Design a pamphlet that could be given to people who have recently moved to the UK. You could include details of British traditions and customs, organisations they may like to join and popular attractions to visit, as well as any other information you feel would be useful for someone who is new to the UK.

Parliament explained

What Parliament does

What happens in Parliament?

The main work of Parliament is to make laws, debate topical issues and look at how our taxes are spent to help run the country. The issues that are discussed in Parliament affect us all: health, the environment, transport, jobs, schools, crime.

Who gets to work in Parliament?

We live in a democratic country, which means we all have a say in how the country is run. We do this by electing Members of Parliament (MPs) to represent our views in the House of Commons. This part of Parliament has the greatest political power. The second part of Parliament is the House of Lords, whose unelected members complement the work of the House of Commons. The third and final part of Parliament is the Monarch, our Queen, who signs the laws that Parliament votes for.

Where is Parliament?

The Houses of Parliament, also known as the Palace of Westminster, is in the centre of London. As well as the home of the UK Parliament, it is also a royal palace and former residence of great kings. The Palace includes many famous sites including the green-coloured House of Commons Chamber and the red-coloured House of Lords Chamber where political decisions are made to this day. It also includes the famous Clock Tower, popularly known as Big Ben.

To give the people of Scotland, Wales and Northern Ireland more say over what happens in their countries, the UK Parliament has devolved (given away) some of its powers to other national and regional bodies. In Scotland, for example, there is the Scottish Parliament which has elected members who make some decisions for Scotland. Wales and Northern Ireland have their own Assemblies and there is also a Greater London Assembly.

Parliament and Government

Are Parliament and Government the same thing?

People often confuse the words 'Parliament' and 'Government' but they are two different things. Not every Member of Parliament is in the Government. The Government is led by the Prime Minister. It is in charge of managing the country and deciding how our taxes are spent. Different government departments run different things. For example, there is a department in charge of health and another in charge of transport. It is the job of everyone in Parliament to check what the Government is doing and to make sure they are doing a good job.

How is the Government formed?

To be in the Government you must belong to the party that received the most votes at election time. This party will therefore have the largest number of Members of Parliament in the House of Commons. The Labour Party received the most votes in the last general election in 2005. Tony Blair was the leader at that time and so he became the Prime Minister. After the election he was asked by the Queen to form his Government. After Tony Blair resigned, the Labour Party agreed that Gordon Brown should take over as Prime Minister.

Parliament explained

You need to be 18 to be able to vote in the UK but voting isn't compulsory. In Australia, however, you face a fine if you don't vote.

Keeping an eye on the Government

All Members of Parliament must check what the Government is doing and how it is spending the money it receives from people when they pay tax. Members of Parliament regularly meet in small groups called Select Committees. These committees can make recommendations to the Government on particular issues such as education, the environment and laws proposed by the European Union (EU).

For example, both the House of Commons and the House of Lords have committees set up to examine laws proposed by the EU. As a member of the EU, the UK agrees it should obey EU laws. Select Committees in both Houses of Parliament play an important role in checking proposals to make sure the likely effects of new EU laws are considered before they are passed.

Select Committee recommendations will be given to the head of the government department in charge of that particular issue. Heads of government departments are called Ministers.

You can see Government Ministers sitting next to the Prime Minister in the House of Commons at Prime Minister's Question Time which happens every Wednesday and is shown on the television and the web.

Every Government Minister has to hold a question and answer session in Parliament on a regular basis. This is usually once every month rather than every week like the Prime Minister. Members of Parliament can use these question times to find out what the Government is doing or suggest ways of doing things better.

> *Parliament has three different parts: The House of Commons, the House of Lords and the Monarch.*

The House of Commons and the House of Lords

Parliament has three different parts: The House of Commons, the House of Lords and the Monarch.

▶ The House of Commons is made up of 646 Members of Parliament (MPs). We vote for our MPs and whoever wins represents everyone in our local area (called a constituency) even if we voted for someone else.

▶ The House of Lords has about 720 members, known as Peers, who are not elected but who have been selected by the Prime Minister and appointed by the Queen.

▶ The Monarch, our Queen, opens and closes Parliament every year, asks the winning party in a General Election to become the Government and officially signs all the laws that Parliament votes for.

How are laws made?

Acts of Parliament are laws of the land that affect us all. For example, laws determine at what age people can drive cars or vote in elections.

A proposed new law is called a Bill. Bills must be agreed by both Houses of Parliament before becoming laws. This often means that a Bill is passed backwards and forwards between the House of Commons and House of Lords, each making changes, until they are both happy with the exact wording. This makes sure that the Bill is properly thought through and that all the consequences of the new law have been considered.

Once both Houses have agreed on the Bill it can be approved by the Queen. This is called Royal Assent and means the Bill becomes an Act of Parliament and therefore officially a new law.

www.parliament.uk

Elections

What is a general election?

Fair and free elections are an essential part of a democracy, allowing the people to have a say in how they want the country to be governed. A general election is held when Parliament is dissolved (closed) by the monarch on the advice of the Prime Minister.

> ❝ **Fair and free elections are an essential part of a democracy, allowing the people to have a say in how they want the country to be governed.** ❞

In the UK, unlike in many other countries such as the USA, we do not have a fixed amount of time between general elections. There is no minimum length of a Parliament but the maximum time is five years, and it is up to the Prime Minister to decide when to hold an election within this period. He or she will hope to choose a time when their party will win again.

Mini glossary

essential – absolutely necessary

impartial – not favouring any political party

bribed – offered money in exchange for something

What happens at election time?

The United Kingdom is divided up into 646 areas called constituencies. We have three main political parties – Conservative, Labour and Liberal Democrats and a number of other smaller parties. Each party that wants to win a constituency will select one person to be their candidate and will try to persuade people to vote for that person and their policies. There may also be independent candidates.

To be a candidate in a general election you must be aged 21 or over and a citizen of Britain, the Commonwealth or the Irish Republic. Some people have jobs where they need to be politically impartial (such as judges, police officers and civil servants) so are disqualified. All candidates must pay a £500 deposit which they will only get back if they secure at least 5% of the votes cast in their constituency.

DID YOU KNOW? In the 2005 general election candidates from 109 registered political parties stood for election. Only nine of these parties succeeded in winning seats. There were also a number of independent candidates, two of whom were elected.

The democracy tree

This tree shows the different layers of democracy that might affect you. Each institution has its own rules and processes for making decisions. On many issues the different institutions have to work together and discuss their decisions with each other.

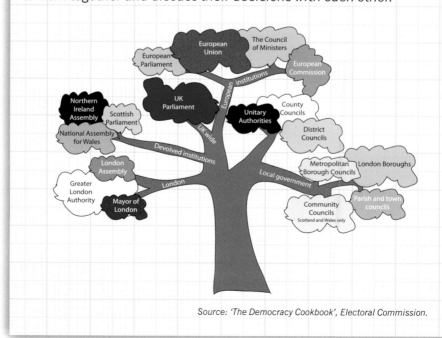

Source: 'The Democracy Cookbook', Electoral Commission.

Elections

Who can vote in parliamentary elections?

To be able to vote you must be aged 18 or over and a British, Irish or Commonwealth citizen. You are not allowed to vote if you are in prison for more than 12 months or in a mental hospital. You must also have your name on the electoral register. Each autumn a registration form is sent to every household for details of those who are, or are about to reach, 18, but you can add your name at any time.

> 66 *To be able to vote you must be aged 18 or over and a British, Irish or Commonwealth citizen.* 99

Voting is not compulsory: you do not have to vote if you do not want to but it is your chance to have your say in how the country is governed. You can vote in person, by post or by proxy (letting someone cast your vote for you).

? *Since 1872 voting has been by secret ballot (in private). This is to stop people from being bribed or threatened into voting for a particular candidate.*

www.parliament.uk

The above information is reprinted with kind permission from UK Parliament.
© Crown copyright

What happens on election (polling) day?

The time between Parliament being dissolved and election day is known as an election campaign. This usually lasts for about three weeks and all of the parties and candidates will try to persuade voters to vote for them by putting up posters, sending out leaflets, knocking on doors and holding meetings.

General elections are usually held on a Thursday. Voting takes place from 07.00 until 22.00 in a number of places throughout each constituency known as polling stations. These are often school and village halls. Each voter has one vote which they cast for the candidate of their choice. The candidate with the largest number of votes becomes the MP for the constituency. This voting system is called 'first-past-the-post'. If a Member dies, retires or is disqualified between elections then a by-election (an election only in the constituency without an MP) is held.

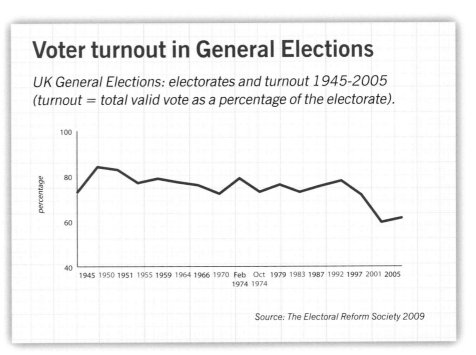

Voter turnout in General Elections

UK General Elections: electorates and turnout 1945-2005 (turnout = total valid vote as a percentage of the electorate).

Source: The Electoral Reform Society 2009

Election jargon buster

Ballot paper

This is the piece of paper you use to make your vote. It shows a list of candidates and voters have to write a cross next to their choice.

Candidate

A person who wants to be elected or has been nominated to be elected is called a candidate.

Canvasser

People who want a candidate to win can help them by becoming a canvasser for their election campaign. A canvasser asks voters who they will vote for and tries to get as many people as possible to vote for their candidate.

Constituency

The UK is divided up into 646 areas called constituencies. The voters in each constituency get to elect one MP to represent the people in their area.

Election campaign

Around election time, candidates and their supporters organise events and activities to convince people that they are the best person to vote for.

Electoral register

Across the UK there are electoral registers: these are lists of all the people who have decided they want to vote at elections. You must have your name on this list before you can vote.

Electorate

This is what we call everyone who is able to vote in an election.

Manifesto

This is something that political parties write around the time of an election, which tells us what they would do if the got elected. A manifesto usually contains pledges (plans of action) on important issues and is often a big part of the election campaign.

MP

At a general election, the people in a constituency (area) can vote to decide who will represent them in Parliament. The person they choose is called a Member of Parliament or an MP.

Parliament

Where new laws are debated and created.

Poll card

This card is sent to everybody who is registered to vote – it has important information about the election like when, where and what time to vote.

Press officer

Press officers work for a candidate or a political party and their job is to tell people working in the media about the candidate's good qualities. Press officers want to get good things about their candidate into the newspapers or on to radio and television.

Spin doctor

Spin doctors help show their candidate in the best light by organising events like photo opportunities with local people.

www.mockelections.co.uk

The above information is reprinted with kind permission from Y-Vote MockElections. © Hansard Society

Allergic to politics?

THE YOUTH CITIZENSHIP COMMISSION was set up to look at ways of developing young people's understanding of citizenship and increasing their participation in politics.

The Commissioners were tasked with finding out what citizenship means to young people, whether they think they should be able to vote at 16 and how our political system can best listen and respond to their concerns. They used the HeadsUp forum to find out what young people up and down the country think about these issues.

There were 394 posts made in the forum from 171 HeadsUp users. This forum was the most popular yet in terms of the number of contributions it received. The discussions on the forum were broad but the general themes and directions of the debate are highlighted below along with the practical suggestions given by forum users.

Politics

HeadsUp users overwhelmingly said that they found politics boring and too complicated. The use of technical terms and long words account for much of this negative feeling.

> 66 There are a lot of words used in politics that makes no sense to us watsoever, they need to get of their high horse and come down to the level that we can understand. 99

The image of Parliament as portrayed in the media emphasised how young people felt politics wasn't for them.

There were many comments that emphasised the connection between politics being relevant (or irrelevant) to young people and their subsequent interest in politics. There was a lot of disagreement about the extent to which politics affects young people, how far up young people's issues are on the political agenda, and therefore whether there was any point being interested or involved. Most of the comments below show a resemblance with the opinions of the electorate at large – young people made it clear that they wouldn't get involved if the issues didn't affect them or they didn't think they had a chance of influencing the outcome.

> 66 It's not that we're not interested it just doesn't directly affect us. A rise in tax, yes we know that sounds bad and yes we know our parents, etc. are going to moan about it but unless you actually pay taxes then you sort of just accept it. 99

A major part of being interested in politics was connected to the ability of young people to effect change or for their ideas to have an outcome. Changing the voting age to 16 was supported by a majority of 3:1 in the forum. Most young people felt that politics might be worthwhile getting involved in and might affect them more if they could vote.

> 66 i just think that we are a bit fustrated because we don't get a say in what our country is like. If young people had a chance to have their say then maybe they would start to like polotics a bit more. 99

Those that were against votes at 16 thought that either 16-year-olds would not have made up their minds enough about politics or were not well-informed enough to be trusted with a vote.

> 66 I know that if I carry on as ignorant as I am about poltics on both a local and national level then when I turn 18 I won't have a clue who to vote for. I don't think that lowering the voting age will be sucessful because 16 year olds are still trying to work out what they believe. 99

Politics in general suffered from an image problem and a misunderstanding of what it involves. The main thing associated with the word politics was old men in suits shouting at each other in Parliament. Issues that were important to young people were not seen as being 'political'.

Allergic to politics?

Politicians

Politicians drew many criticisms from young people for being out of touch, not listening, not speaking simply enough, setting a bad example, not visiting young people and blaming them for all society's ills!

> 66 It is believed politicians do not pay attention to us young people. They look down on us and point the finger at us whenever something is going wrong in the comuunity. Politicians should walk with us and involve us someway. 99

Young people felt that politicians also needed to be more representative of the population as a whole in order to appeal to voters and young people.

> 66 i belive young people are rather fed up with the politics sorounding them than a lack of interest becuase recently we saw a vast number of young involved in the US presidential election. So i think we need a change in our male dominate and instituionally racist Britian. 99

In terms of how they would like to be contacted by politicians, young people overall were keen on their MPs being on MySpace or Bebo. A majority of 2:1 said they thought it was a good idea. They felt that this would give them a better understanding of what their politicians were like and would allow them to stay in contact more effectively.

> 66 I do think that our MP should be on myspace because, many young people use it and if an MP does, it would show that he is with the trends and is able to comunicate with young people in a way that they would actually listen… children may also start to think differently about MPs' and politics, they may start to think that they are not all boring poeple who do not understand kids and start thinking that they can be child friendly. Children respect and listen to them more. 99

However there were also those that felt MPs on social networking sites could be a little embarrassing or might be invading young people's space (although usually social networking sites do require consent from users before any contact is made).

> 66 I don't think that MP's on MySpace etc will work at all, politicians seem so desperate to be 'down with the kids' and thought of as 'cool' and representative of today's youth rather than concerned with the actual issues that affect them. I would rather vote for someone who will fight for our rights and support our issues rather than someone who can speak in slang and write in text type on facebook. 99

There was also support for politicians leaving Westminster and coming to where young people are to explain how politics works or to update them with what they are currently doing to improve the local area.

> 66 Children are put off by politics because all you ever see on the news is old people talking in the House of Lords of The House of Commons. Politicians should go into school or youth centres and talk about what they want in their local area. They should make it less formal and talk about that matters which affect everyday children. 99

Media and information

The media was widely blamed by young people for making Parliament and politics seem much more complicated than it needed to be. It was also criticised for its negative portrayal of young people and politicians.

> 66 I think There Should Be More Press On The Good Things Goverment Do Because ifind The Mistakes Or Bad Remarks Are High-lighted In Our Local Papers And Our Favourite Television Chanels. 99

Allergic to politics?

> 66 When it comes to young people they dont understand the current worlds circumstances they just think its the lack of role models but think about it who is our role model its the government!! and we all know that because we hear about it more in the current news than anywhere else and if we keep on hearing criticism we will think they are not doing anything about the crisis in the world eg. the bombings in india. or the credit crunch 99

They almost universally complained about the lack of clear, simple information available for young people and this exacerbated the idea that politics wasn't for them or that adults were purposefully excluding them from politics. HeadsUp users had plenty of ideas about how they would like to be more informed or learn about politics. TV seemed to be the most favoured medium and many were keen on seeing more political debates on TV that involved politicians and celebrities.

Advertising politics to young people and how important it is was also highlighted by many of users in the forum.

> 66 To get teenagers more interested in politics I think it should be advertised like everything else. Bring it to everyone's attention how important politics is and how is affects EVERYONE, so we all might as well have our say. There should be more sites like this [HeadsUp], TV shows too. 99

Citizenship lessons

There appeared to be little awareness that citizenship was compulsory in secondary schools or that it was linked to politics, as more political education was one of the solutions regularly suggested by young people to combat apathy or ignorance.

> 66 If there were lessons in Citizenship based specifically on politics, it would increase our understanding of it. 99

Defining citizenship

HeadsUp users were less likely to see citizenship as something given to everyone as a right and more in terms of the duties citizenship entails to wider society. This was evident in their definitions of being a good citizen as not breaking the law, being environmentally friendly and helping others wherever possible. The feeling of community, attachment to their local area and all citizens being linked through citizenship was particularly strong.

> 66 A citizen means that you are united with everyone else in your neighbourhood and you be friendly with each other it also means to abide by the laws that the government passes and that you should not be a criminal as this breaks down communities 99

Equality, respect and a multicultural society without discrimination were also seen as synonymous with British citizenship.

> 66 Citizenship in Britain has changed over the years as more and more people have moved here. I think it means that no matter what your race, beliefs or culture is you are still a part of the country and no one should tell you otherwise because of your differences. 99

Mini glossary

overwhelmingly – *having a large majority*

relevant – *meaningful*

exacerbated – *increased; made worse*

apathy – *lack of interest*

synonymous – *meaning the same thing; closely associated with*

www.hansardsociety.org.uk

Information from the Hansard Society. © Hansard Society

Got a taste for it?

THERE ARE LOTS OF WAYS to get involved in democracy throughout the year, not just at election time.

If you want to have your views heard on an issue you care about you could:

▶ submit a petition;

▶ write a letter to your local representative;

▶ provide evidence to a committee;

▶ get your representative to ask a question on your behalf;

▶ get involved in a youth council or youth parliament; or

▶ start a local campaign.

Submit a petition

A petition is a list of names and basic details of people that support a particular issue or campaign. They are normally used to draw attention to a cause. Petitions highlight the level of support for the cause locally, nationally or internationally.

You may be approached on the street and asked to sign a petition. This is a very basic way of becoming involved in the political process. Many petitions are also distributed by email or on a website, which obviously has some practical advantages over standing on street corners!

If you are campaigning on a particular issue you may decide that you want to formally submit a petition to the UK Parliament or another democratic body. To do this you need to follow special guidelines.

Write to or email your representatives

By writing to your representatives you are making them aware of what you think about an issue. Most representatives look at all letters and emails from the people they represent. The more people who write to a representative on a particular issue, the more they will sit up and take notice.

Before you write, find out which of your representatives is responsible for the issue you are concerned about. Make it clear in your letter or email what action you would like your representative to take.

Get your representative to ask an 'official' question

All MPs, MSPs, AMs and MLAs have the right to ask or 'table' questions to government ministers and departments. You can write to your representative and request that they ask a question addressing your concerns.

There are two main forms of questions in the UK Parliament:

▶ questions for oral (spoken) answers; and

▶ questions for written answers.

About 50,000 of these 'parliamentary questions' are raised each year.

In the House of Commons, oral questions are asked during an official 'Question Time' which takes place for an hour on Mondays, Tuesdays, Wednesdays and Thursdays. There is a limit to the number of oral questions that can be asked, but MPs can ask a larger number of written questions. Questions are usually answered in seven working days.

This is a good way to get your views heard and to get a specific answer to what may be a complicated issue. It may take some time however. Your MP may get a lot of requests to ask questions, or the department that has to be asked may not be answering again for a while. It pays to be patient!

Give evidence to an official committee

Committees are the part of our democratic institutions that investigate issues in-depth. To do this they gather evidence and make recommendations. It is possible for you or your youth organisation to give evidence to a committee to let them know your views on the issues they are investigating.

Got a taste for it?

Committees will invite 'experts' to give 'oral' evidence. This means sitting in front of the committee members and answering their questions. For example, children and young people were able to provide their views on children's rights to a UK Parliament select committee on Human Rights.

It is only possible for a limited number of people to give evidence in person so committees also ask for written evidence. Some committees also run discussion forums on a website so you can make your views known online. To find out what issues are currently being investigated keep an eye on the institution websites:

► www.parliament.uk;

► www.scottishparliament.uk;

► www.wales.gov.uk; or

► www.niassembly.gov.uk.

Get involved in a youth forum or youth council

Your local youth forum is somewhere you can let off steam about the things that you care about. It also gives you access to the people who help make decisions about your local area. The organisations are an extension of the formal institutions of democracy and allow young people from all walks of life to come together on common issues.

Local councils are currently committed to providing opportunities for young people to put forward their views. Look out for advertisements in your local area, in your local paper or get in touch with your local authority for more details.

What is being a youth mayor all about?

Lewisham's first ever youth mayor, 17-year-old Manny Hawkes, talks about his achievements.

'I like to know what's going on around me so when I heard about the opportunity to run as youth mayor I couldn't resist. I had to get 30 young people from Lewisham to nominate me. The council then gave all the people running for youth mayor election training, which taught us how to get our ideas across clearly.

As youth mayor I'm not in charge of young people, but I advise the council on how to best serve young people in the borough. I work with a youth advisory group made up of people aged 11 to 25. We have a budget of £25,000 which we get to spend on services for young people.

Things that we've got off the ground include:

► setting up a rehearsal space for bands;

► running community safety workshops for young people that showed people how to develop self-awareness and deal with the fear of crime;

► a directory of services – there are lots of services for young people in Lewisham, but people were unaware of what they are;

► setting up the 'be involved' website – this is a direct feed into democracy where young people can access members of the council or the youth advisory group; and

► running a 10 x 10 over cricket tournament for primary schools.

It's taken a while to get things happening. Working with the council requires patience because things happen slowly. You just need a bit of assertiveness and willpower. When I first started I was more laid back, but now I say 'I want this done and I want it done now!' If you can be bothered to get something done, other people will see what you do and want to get involved as well.

My advice to young people is that if you have a problem with something in your area or a problem with how the country is being run, you can't complain if you can't be bothered to do something about it. Politics affects all of us and it's not going to go away by ignoring it.'

www.dopolitics.org.uk

The above information is an extract from The Democracy Cookbook. For more, visit the Do Politics Centre, the Electoral Commission's idea and resource hub for democracy practitioners: www.dopolitics.org.uk.
© The Electoral Commission

The case for votes at 16

OVER 1.5 MILLION 16- AND 17-YEAR-OLDS are denied the vote in the United Kingdom. For years there has been a consistent demand from young people for votes at 16, and a clear case for change. That case is now overwhelming.

At 16, we can leave school, work full time and pay taxes, leave home, get married, join the armed forces, and make lots of decisions about our future.

At 16, people become adults and take control of their own futures – so why can't we have the basic right of all adult citizens of a say in how the country is run?

We're all interested in issues; from climate change to racism, from education to crime. Voting is the fundamental way that we have our say on issues, and we think that at 16, young people are mature enough to be properly listened to.

Stopping 16- and 17-year-olds from voting and having the chance to be heard sends a signal to them and to society, especially politicians, that our views aren't valid and that we aren't real citizens. At a time when people feel that politics isn't relevant to them, young people need to be encouraged to take part in democracy, not kept out from it.

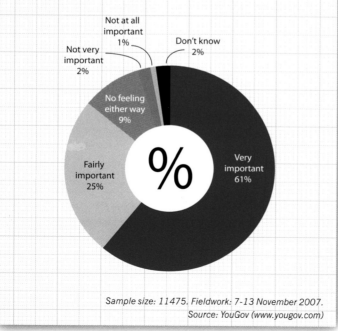

How important is political engagement?

Respondents were asked: 'Thinking about how Britain SHOULD BE – and not necessarily the way things are today – how important would you say it is that everyone votes in general elections?'

Not at all important 1%
Don't know 2%
Not very important 2%
No feeling either way 9%
Fairly important 25%
%
Very important 61%

Sample size: 11475. Fieldwork: 7-13 November 2007.
Source: YouGov (www.yougov.com)

Citizenship education, youth engagement campaigns and high-speed interactive media have made this generation the most politically aware and educated ever, but the number of people taking part in politics just keeps on dropping. It's time we recognised the abilities of 16-year-olds, including them in society and showing them the trust and respect that society expects of them.

It's time we gave young people the basic right of any citizen – the right to vote.

www.votesat16.org.uk

The above information is reprinted with kind permission from Votes at 16.
© Votes at 16

 A Youth Citizenship Commission's consultation found that 66% of respondents backed lowering the voting age to 16.

Votes at 16?

IN AN ATTEMPT TO ENGAGE YOUNG PEOPLE with the formal political process, the Youth Citizenship Commission (YCC) – a body set up as part of the Governance of Britain agenda to 'examine ways of developing young people's understanding of citizenship and increase their participation in politics' – is beginning a three-month consultation on lowering the voting age to 16 – the first of a range of proposals.

The consultation paper includes information on where we fit in internationally, the current legal picture (what rights and responsibilities come into effect at what ages) and the implications of both leaving the law untouched and reforming it.

16-year-olds can get married, have children and join the army. They are among those who will feel the long term impact of global warming, our foreign policy and the recent financial crisis. They will face major challenges from rising unemployment and will feel the full effects of our education policy.

On the face of it, then, it seems logical that the voting age should be lowered. However, if young people are disillusioned by and uninterested in parliamentary politics, giving them the option of voting as a lone measure can't possibly solve the deeper problem. The right 18-year-olds have to vote does not ensure a reasonable turn-out amongst that age group and, once the novelty has worn off, what would ensure reasoned and regular voting from the under-18s?

At 16 a small proportion of people are highly politically aware and active, but equally there are those who can't even name a single party or minister.

I sat through four years of compulsory Citizenship education, and my political interest and activism exists very much despite it. Like many other schools, mine rolled the lesson in with PSHCE lessons (ed. – that's Personal, Social, Health and Community Education for those unfamiliar with the latest pre-16 curriculum!) leaving a vast range of content to be covered in just an hour a week. The teacher was not a specialist and was ill-prepared both for the content and for the appalling behaviour of some of the class. Many teachers do not take the subject seriously, and few students see it as anything other than an extra hour a week to chat with mates. To be at all effective more resources and creative thinking is needed. Don't just talk about community participation – get the students involved, have field trips, invite guest speakers in, have debates. Do anything other than sit in a room and plough through worksheets.

 A single measure like votes at 16 won't get the job done. 99

A single measure like votes at 16 won't get the job done. Citizenship education must be drastically redesigned and embedded into the wider syllabus before we have any hope of producing 16-year-olds, and adults, who are willing to engage in the political process.

21 October 2008

Mini glossary

disillusioned – *disappointed by; having lost faith in*

novelty – *something that is interesting because it is new or different*

syllabus – *course of study followed at school*

www.opendemocracy.net

Young people can vote from the age of 16 in Austria, Brazil, Cuba, Nicaragua and the Isle of Man.

This article was originally published in the independent online magazine www.opendemocracy.net © openDemocracy.net

Activities

Brainstorm

Brainstorm to find out what you know about democracy in action.

1. What are the three different parts of Parliament? Give a brief explanation of each part.

   ....

   ....

   ....

2. What is the difference between Parliament and Government?

   ....

   ....

Oral activities

3. As a class, hold a mock election to decide who you would elect to make decisions in your school. Divide into three groups, with each group deciding what their main policies will be. Each group should present their policies to the rest of the class and answer any questions people may have about how they would govern the school. Once each group has presented, take a vote by secret ballot to find out which group has the most votes and has won the election.

   NOTES..

   ....

   ....

4. In two groups, debate the motion 'This house believes that the voting age should be lowered to 16,' with one group arguing for the motion and the other arguing against it.

Moral Dilemmas

5. Some people think that a democratic government should not include a monarch or a House of Lords, as they have not been elected by the people. Do you think the Royal Family and the House of Lords should make up part of Parliament? Why, or why not?

6. Making voting in General Elections compulsory is one suggestion for tackling low voter turnout. What might the concerns be when considering such a measure? Do you think voting is a right or a responsibility?

Activities

Research activities

7. Find out about the policies of the main political parties in the UK. Based on your research, decide which party you would vote for in a General Election. Which policies do you feel are most important for young people to consider?

   CONCLUSIONS ....

   ....

   ....

   ....

   ....

8. Investigate youth councils and forums in your local area. How easy is it to find out about getting involved in politics in your area? Make a list of suggestions for how you could promote youth councils and encourage people to get involved.

   NOTES ....

   ....

   ....

   ....

Written activities

Complete the following activities in your exercise books or on a sheet of paper.

9. Choose a political party in the UK and create a catchy slogan you feel conveys their main concerns.

10. Read the article *Got a taste for it?* on pages 22-23. Come up with a question you would like your representative to ask concerning an issue you care about.

Design activities

11. Create a poster to get young people interested and involved in politics. Use your poster to emphasise how politics affect young people and to advertise how people can get involved. Use the article *Got a taste for it?* on pages 22-23 as a starting point.

Key Facts

▶ In its simplest meaning, 'citizenship' is used to refer to the status of being a citizen – that is, to being a member of a particular political community or state. (page 1)

▶ The main driver of a feeling of attachment or belonging to Britain is age, with younger people being less strongly attached to Britain. (page 3)

▶ Figures from the latest citizenship survey show that 82 per cent of people see their community as cohesive, an increase from 80 per cent in 2005. (page 4)

▶ Addressing deprivation and how people connect is more important for social cohesion than trying to get everyone to adhere to the same fixed notion of 'Britishness'. This is according to research published by the Joseph Rowntree Foundation. (page 6)

▶ Around half (51%) of respondents in the Britain and Beyond survey carried out by YouthNet said they feel European; however, the vast majority (74%) thought that the UK was very different to the rest of Europe. (page 7)

▶ Since 1 November 2005 everyone that wants to permanently live in the UK has to take a test or attend citizenship and language classes to prove that they know about life in the UK. (page 11)

▶ The main work of Parliament is to make laws, debate topical issues and look at how our taxes are spent to help run the country. The issues that are discussed in Parliament affect us all: health, the environment, transport, jobs, schools and crime. (page 14)

▶ Parliament has three different parts: The House of Commons, the House of Lords and the Monarch. (page 15)

▶ Fair and free elections are an essential part of a democracy, allowing the people to have a say in how they want the country to be governed. (page 16)

▶ Voting is not compulsory: you do not have to vote if you do not want to but it is your chance to have your say in how the country is governed. (page 17)

▶ Voter turnout in general elections has dropped to record lows in recent years. (page 17)

▶ Users of the HeadsUp forum overwhelmingly said that they found politics boring and too complicated. The use of technical terms and long words account for much of this negative feeling. The image of Parliament as portrayed in the media emphasised how young people felt politics wasn't for them. (page 19)

▶ You must be 18 or over to be able to vote in parliamentary elections in the United Kingdom. (page 24)

Glossary

Allegiance – The loyalty citizens owe to their country.

'Britishness' – The term 'Britishness' refers to our national identity. There is much debate about what British values and identities are or should be, and whether they are still relevant.

Citizenship – 'Citizenship' refers to the status of being a citizen (a member of a particular political community or state). However, it is a broad term which also refers to the behaviour and actions of a citizen. In terms of an educational activity, citizenship is the process of helping people become active and responsible citizens.

Civic – Relating to citizens.

Cohesion – The bonds that hold members of a community together. Social cohesion occurs when a society works together for shared values.

Constituency – The UK is divided up into 646 areas which are called constituencies. The voters in each constituency get to elect one MP to represent the people in their area in Parliament.

Democracy – A system in which everyone living in a country has a say who runs that country.

Devolution – When the Government gives away some of its powers to other national and regional bodies to give them more say over what happens in their countries.

Diversity – Accepting and respecting differences between and within different groups.

Election – A vote which is held to choose someone to hold public office or another position. A general election is when people decide which MP will represent them in Parliament.

Electorate – Everyone who is able to vote in an election.

First-past-the-post – The system used to decide the winners of elections in the UK. This means that each voter has one vote and whichever candidate within their constituency gets the most votes becomes the MP for that region.

Immigration – Moving to another country to live there permanently.

Integration – Incorporating a racial or religious group in a community.

Houses of Parliament – The Houses of Parliament are the House of Commons and the House of Lords, which are in Westminster Palace in London.

Mock election – Mock elections are sometimes held among young people who are not eligible to vote in national elections in order to find out about their political opinions.

MP – MP stands for Member of Parliament. MPs represent constituencies in the UK and meet in the House of Commons to debate issues and make decisions.

Multiculturalism – A society which is made up of a number of groups with different customs and beliefs.

Parliament – Many people confuse Parliament and Government. However, while the job of the Government is to run the country, the job of Parliament is to check what the Government is doing and that they are doing a good job. Parliament has three different parts: the House of Commons, the House of Lords and the Monarch. The main work of Parliament is to make laws, debate topical issues and look at how our taxes are spent in running the country.

Turnout – Refers to the number of people in the UK who are allowed to vote and who actually turn out to vote in elections.